THE WORLD OF PLANTS

HOW DO PLANTS MAKE AND SPREAD THEIR SEEDS?

by Ruth Owen

PowerKiDS press™

New York

Published in 2015 by The Rosen Publishing Group, Inc.
29 East 21st Street, New York, NY 10010

First Edition

Produced for Rosen by Ruby Tuesday Books Ltd
Editor for Ruby Tuesday Books Ltd: Mark J. Sachner
US Editor: Joshua Shadowens
Designer: Emma Randall

Photo Credits:
Cover, 1, 4, 6–7, 8–9, 10–11, 13, 14 (bottom), 15 (top), 16, 17, 18–19, 20–21, 22–23, 24–25, 26–27, 28–29 © Shutterstock; 5, 14 (top), 15 (bottom right) © FLPA; 12, 15 (bottom left) © Wikipedia Creative Commons; 17 (top) © Science Photo Library.

Library of Congress Cataloging-in-Publication Data

Owen, Ruth, 1967–
 How do plants make and spread their seeds? / by Ruth Owen. — First edition.
    pages cm. — (The world of plants)
 Includes index.
 ISBN 978-1-4777-7145-7 (library binding) — ISBN 978-1-4777-7146-4 (pbk.) —
ISBN 978-1-4777-7147-1 (6-pack)
1. Seeds—Juvenile literature. 2. Seeds—Dispersal—Juvenile literature. I. Title.
II. Series: World of plants (New York, N.Y.)
 QK661.O94 2015
 581.4′67—dc23

2014010912

Manufactured in the United States of America

CPSIA Compliance Information: Batch #WS14PK8: For Further Information contact Rosen Publishing, New York, New York at 1-800-237-9932.

Contents

Seeds, Big and Small

Peanuts, corn kernels, acorns, kidney beans. What do all these things have in common? They are are all types of **seeds**.

Some seeds, like those produced by orchids, are so tiny they look like specks of dust. Others grow much larger. In fact, the largest seeds on Earth are the size of a basketball. These enormous seeds, which come from the coco de mer palm tree, often weigh up to 40 pounds (18 kg) each!

Large or small, every seed contains all the material needed to grow a new plant. Most seeds form inside flowers. Some grow inside **cones**.

So how do plants grow their seeds? And how does a seed make the journey from its parent plant to its eventual growing place?

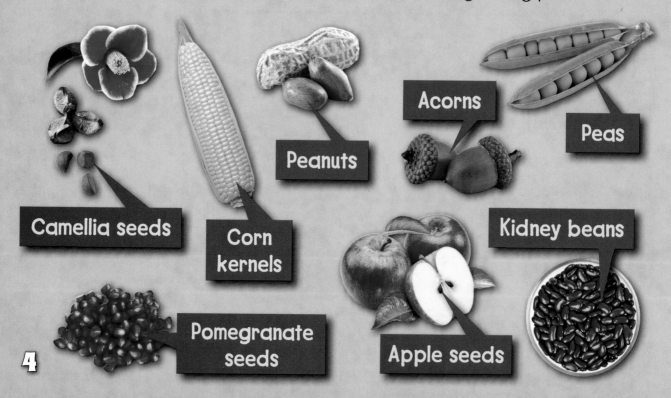

Camellia seeds

Corn kernels

Peanuts

Acorns

Peas

Kidney beans

Pomegranate seeds

Apple seeds

Marigold seeds

Coco de mer
palm tree seed

Making Seeds

The seeds of many plants, including many species of trees, grow inside flowers.

A flower has male parts called **stamens**. Each stamen is made up of a filament and an **anther**. The female part of a flower is called the **pistil**. Each pistil is made up of a **stigma**, a stalk called a style, and an **ovary**. Making seeds begins with **pollination** of a plant's flowers. The **pollen** made by the anthers of one flower must be carried to the stigma of another flower of the same species. Pollen can be carried from flower to flower by the wind or on the body of an animal, such as a bee.

A bee covered with yellow pollen

Once a flower has been pollinated, the next stage in making seeds is fertilzation. A pollen grain on the flower's stigma sends a tiny tube down the style into the flower's ovary. Inside the ovary are **ovules**, which are tiny plant parts that can become seeds. The pollen tube pierces an ovule and fertilizes it. Now the ovule can grow into a seed.

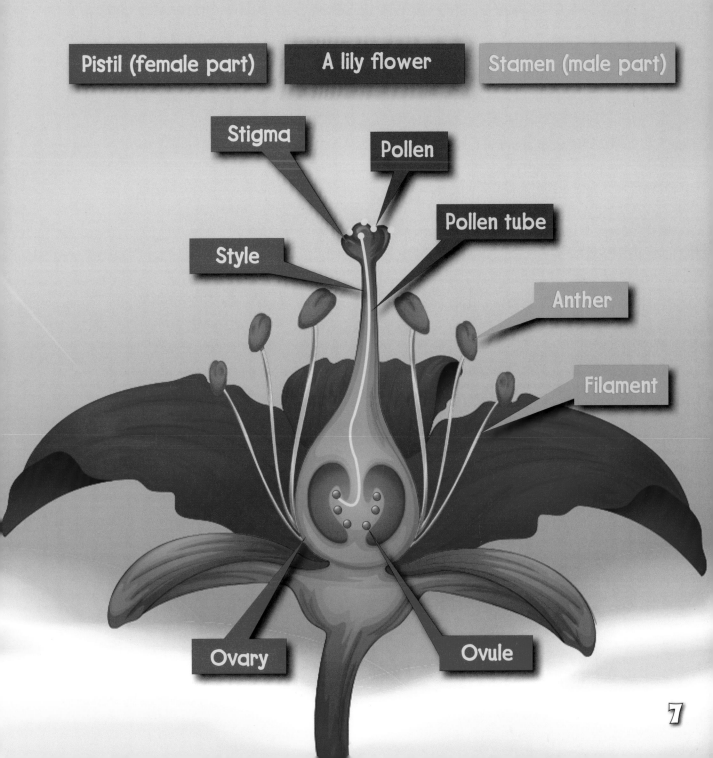

Pistil (female part)

A lily flower

Stamen (male part)

Stigma

Pollen

Pollen tube

Style

Anther

Filament

Ovary

Ovule

Protective Fruits

Once a flower has been pollinated and fertilization has taken place, the flower's seeds start to grow inside its ovary.

As the seeds grow, the flower's ovary swells and changes to become a protective case, or covering, called a fruit. As the fruit forms, the flower shrivels and dies.

When we use the word "fruit" we think of an apple, peach, or cherry. A fruit, however, is any kind of outer layer that protects seeds as they grow. Some seeds are protected by soft fruits, such as tomatoes or oranges. Other seeds, such as poppy seeds, grow in hard fruits called capsules or seedpods.

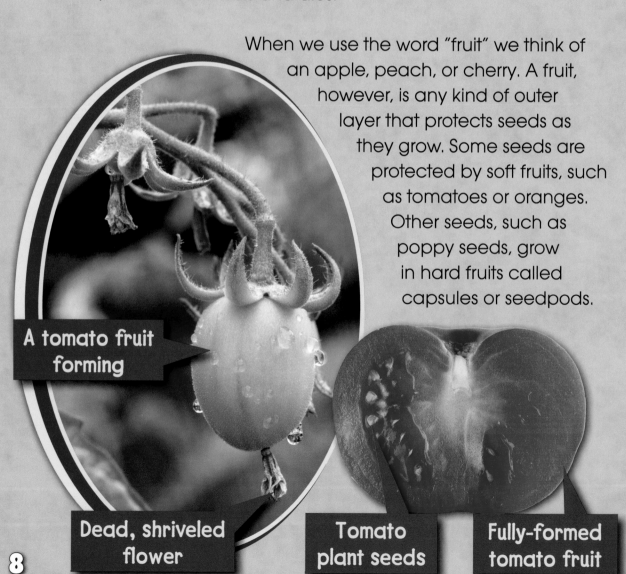

A tomato fruit forming

Dead, shriveled flower

Tomato plant seeds

Fully-formed tomato fruit

Fully formed
poppy seedpod

Poppy

A seedpod
forming

Seeds Up Close

Some types of flowers produce a small number of seeds. Others may produce hundreds or even thousands of seeds.

Seeds look very different, but they have the same parts. The outside of a seed is covered by a protective outer layer called the seed coat. Inside a seed is a tiny new plant called an **embryo**. Packed around the embryo is a food supply, called the endosperm. This food supply helps the new plant grow.

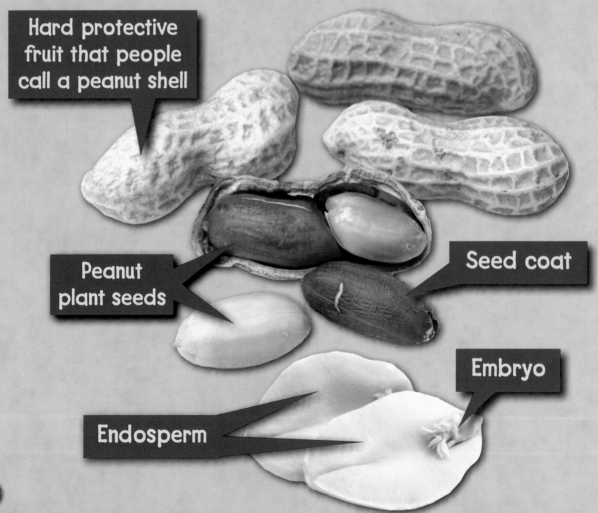

Hard protective fruit that people call a peanut shell

Peanut plant seeds

Seed coat

Endosperm

Embryo

The endosperm of some seeds, such as bean plant seeds, look like tiny leaves. They are called cotyledons or seed leaves. When a new plant emerges from the soil, it's these seed leaves that appear first. The seed leaves continue to feed the tiny, new plant until it grows actual leaves and begins to make its own food.

leaves

Bean seeds

Cotyledons (or seed leaves)

Seed coat

New bean plant

What Does a Seed Need?

Once a plant's seeds are fully grown, they must leave the parent plant.

In order to stand a chance of successfully growing into a new plant, most seeds need soil, sunlight, water, and **nutrients**.

If a new plant, called a seedling, tries to grow in the ground close to its parent plant, however, there may be too much competition between the seedling, the bigger plant, and even other seedlings. As the young plant grows larger, there may not be enough water and nutrients in the soil to go around. The parent plant may block out sunlight. Therefore, it's important for many types of seeds that they move to new growing places away from their parent plants. How does this happen?

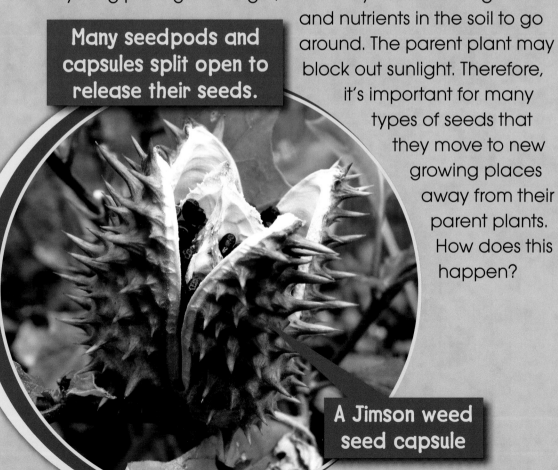

Many seedpods and capsules split open to release their seeds.

A Jimson weed seed capsule

Soft fruits fall from their parent plants and then rot on the ground to release their seeds.

Seeds on the Move

Many seeds are moved to new growing places inside animals!

The protective outer fruits of many seeds become food for animals. Birds, bears, monkeys, and even elephants feed on fruit and also eat the seeds inside the fruit. The animal's body digests the soft fruit, but hard seeds can pass through an animal's **digestive system** unharmed. The seeds then leave the animal's body in its waste and land in a new growing place—often far from the parent plant.

Black bear droppings containing seeds and undigested berries

A robin eating berries

Marula tree

Elephants feed on the fruit and seeds of the marula tree. It can take more than 24 hours for the seeds to leave the large animal's body in its dung. In this time, an elephant may have walked miles (km) from the parent marula tree.

Marula fruits

Marula seeds in elephant dung

Burying Seeds

When nuts, acorns, and other seeds fall from plants in the fall, there are lots of hungry animals waiting to move these seeds from place to place.

Chipmunks collect seeds and store them underground in their burrows. During the winter months, which chipmunks spend underground, they feed on this stored food. Not every seed gets eaten, though, and some of the leftover chipmunk food may grow into new plants.

A chipmunk can store thousands of seeds each fall.

Some plants produce seeds with a rich food treat called an elaiosome. Many species of ants collect these seeds and feed the elaiosome to their **larvae**. The rest of the seed is then discarded in the ants' underground nest and may grow into a new plant.

Seed

Elaiosome

Squirrels store acorns for winter by burying them. Some of these seeds grow into new oak trees.

Hooks and Spikes

The fruits and seeds of some plants grow hooks or spikes that help them hitch a ride to new growing places.

The flowers of the burdock plant produce balls of seeds called burrs. Each seed in a burr is armed with a tiny hook. When an animal brushes past the burr, the seeds' hooks attach to the animal's fur or feathers. The seed ball is then pulled from its stem and takes a ride away from its parent plant.

A burdock plant

A burdock burr

Nicknamed puncture vines, the caltrop plant family produces woody fruits with spikes, or barbs, that look like medieval weapons. The spikes of these fruits can push through skin, clothes, and shoes, and have been known to puncture bicycle tires!

A water caltrop fruit

A cow covered with burrs

Blown by the Wind

Some plants have developed seeds that use the wind to move to new places.

Many seeds that are **dispersed** by the wind are tiny and light. Larger, heavier wind-dispersed seeds have wings or other adaptations to help them stay up in the air for as long as possible. This is important because the longer a seed is floating on the wind, the farther from its parent plant it can travel. Maple tree seeds have wings, like helicopter blades, that help the seeds spin through the air.

Wing

Maple tree seed

A dandelion flower can produce up to 400 seeds. Each seed has a fluffy parachute that catches the wind and helps the seed float to a new growing place.

Dandelion flower

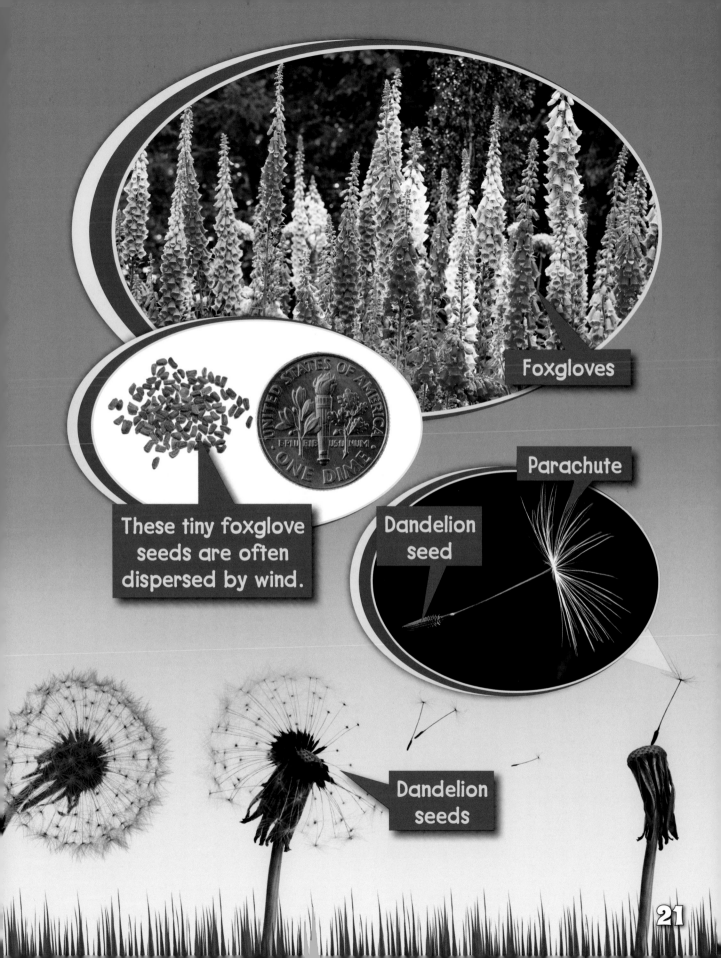

Foxgloves

These tiny foxglove seeds are often dispersed by wind.

Parachute

Dandelion seed

Dandelion seeds

Moving in Water

The seeds of plants that grow near rivers or the ocean may be spread by water to new growing places.

Pond irises grow near ponds, lakes, and rivers. When the seedpods of iris flowers split open, the seeds fall into the water. The seeds can then be carried long distances until they become embedded in some mud and start to grow in a new place.

Seedpod

Pond iris seeds

Pond irises

The seeds of some types of palm trees grow inside fruits called coconuts. When these fruits fall from trees that are growing on beaches, they may be carried out to sea. In time, the coconuts are washed up on a different beach, where they can begin to grow in the sand, many miles (km) from their parent tree.

Coconut fruit

Palm tree seedling

Palm trees

Palm tree seed

Hairy seed coat

Seeds from Cones

Not all plants produce flowers. Many species of trees, including pine trees, grow their seeds inside cones.

Like the male and female parts of a flower, pine trees have male and female cones. Male cones produce pollen, which they release into the air. Female cones produce ovules, which are tucked away between their woody, overlapping scales.

Pollen from male pinecones settles on a female cone's scales and fertilizes the ovules. The ovules then develop into seeds. Once the seeds are fully grown, the scales of the female cone open out fully to allow the seeds to fall to the ground.

Pollen

Male pine cone

Female pinecone that's still forming

Open female pinecone

Scales

Seeds

Pine tree seeds

Hard seed coat

25

Tiny Seed, Big Potential!

Seeds can be big, small, round, oval, disc-shaped, lumpy, long and thin, shiny or rough. No matter what its size or shape, a seed has the potential to become a new plant.

Most seeds ripen in summer and then separate from their parent plant. Once the seeds are settled in some soil, they wait for spring before starting to grow.

Some plants grow in just a few weeks, produce flowers and seeds, and then die. Others, like giant sequoia trees, may continue to grow for centuries. It's amazing to think that the largest living thing on Earth, the General Sherman giant sequoia, has been growing for more than 2,000 years. And it all began with a tiny seed not much bigger than a grain of rice!

Giant sequoia cone

Giant sequoia seeds

The General Sherman
giant sequoia tree

Investigating the World of Plants

INVESTIGATION 1: Protective Cones

The scales on the female cones of a pine tree can open and close. When it rains, the scales close up to protect the cone's seeds from water. See this in action in the following investigation.

You will need:
- A pinecone with open scales
- A jar with a screw-top lid
- Water

Step 1:
Place the cone inside the jar.

Step 4:
Once the cone's scales are tightly closed, remove the cone from the water and place it in a warm, sunny spot to dry out. Keep watch for what happens next.

Step 2:
Fill the jar with water so that the cone is completely submerged, and then screw on the lid.

Step 3:
Keep watch on the cone to see its scales closing.

Why? How? What?
What do you think will happen as the cone gets dry?
(See page 32 for the answer.)

INVESTIGATION 2:

Seedling Competition

Seeds move away from their parent plants to new growing places to avoid competition for resources such as sunlight, water, and nutrients. In this investigation, find out what happens if a seedling has too much competition.

Step 1:

Use the scissors to pierce three holes in the bottom of each yogurt carton (to allow water to drain through). Label the cartons A and B.
(Only use scissors if an adult is there to help you.)

Step 2:

Fill each carton three-quarters full with potting soil.

Step 3:

Place five bean seeds on top of the soil in carton A and two bean seeds in carton B. Cover the seeds with more soil, put each carton on a saucer, and then place the cartons in a sunny spot.

Step 4:

Give each carton half a cup of water every other day. The potting soil will contain the nutrients the seedlings need.

Step 5:

When the bean seedlings emerge, remove the weakest-looking seedling from carton B to leave the strongest seedling growing with no competition. Watch how the seedlings grow.

Why? How? What?

Which carton do you think will contain the healthiest plant?

What is happening to the seedlings in carton A?

(See page 32 for the answer.)

anthers (AN-thurz)
The parts of a flower that produce pollen.

cones (KOHNZ)
Organs on some non-flowering plants that produce either the pollen or ovules needed for making seeds.

digestive system (dy-JES-tiv SIS-tem)
The group of body parts, including the stomach and intestines, that break down food so that a body can use it for fuel.

dispersed (dih-SPERST)
Spread over a wide area.

embryo (EM-bree-oh)
In plant science, the part of a seed that develops into a plant.

larvae (LAHR-vee)
The young of many types of insects. A larva hatches from an egg.

nutrients (NOO-tree-ents)
Substances needed by a plant or animal to help it live and grow. Plants take in nutrients from the soil using their roots. The nutrients in soil are dissolved in water.

ovary (OH-vuh-ree) The part of a flower where its seeds form.

ovules (AHV-yuhlz) Tiny parts of a plant that become seeds when fertilized by pollen.

pistil (PIS-tuhl) The female reproductive part of a flower. The pistil is made up of the ovary, the style, and the stigma.

pollen (PAH-lin)
A colored dust made on the anthers of flowers, which plants need in order to reproduce.

pollination (pah-lih-NAY-shun)
When pollen is moved from the anthers of one flower to the stigma of another.

potential (poh-TEN-shul) The qualities or abilities that may be developed into something useful or successful in the future.

seeds (SEEDZ) Parts of a plant that contain all the material needed to grow a new plant.

species (SPEE-sheez) One type of living thing. The members of a species look alike and can reproduce together.

stamens (STAY-munz) The male parts of a flower. Each stamen is made up of a filament and an anther.

stigma (STIG-muh) The part of a flower where pollen must land in order for pollination to happen so that a flower can begin to make seeds.

Websites

Due to the changing nature of Internet links, PowerKids Press has developed an online list of websites related to the subject of this book. This site is updated regularly. Please use this link to access the list:

www.powerkidslinks.com/wop/seeds/

Read More

Dickmann, Nancy. *A Bean's Life*. Mankato, MN: Capstone Press, 2011.

Rhodes, Evan. *How Do Seeds Sprout?* New York: Gareth Stevens, 2013.

Thomson, Ruth. *The Life Cycle of an Oak Tree*. New York: PowerKids Press, 2009.

Index

Answers

INVESTIGATION 1:
As the pinecone dries out, its scales will open out again. This is exactly what a pinecone does once it stops raining.

INVESTIGATION 2:
It's likely that the seedling in carton B will grow faster and look more healthy than the seedlings in carton A. The seedlings in carton A are weaker because they are competing for water and nutrients.